Teenage Thoughts of Hope

By

Morongwa Hope Moagi

Teenage Thoughts of Hope

Teenage Thoughts of Hope

Edited and Published by
William Jenkins
4036 Pine Street
Burnaby BC V5G 1Z5 Canada
williamhenryjenkins@gmail.com
http://williamjenkins.ca
Telephone: 1-604-685-4136

ISBN: Paperback 978-1-928164-37-1
ISBN: Electronic Book 978-1-928164-38-8
Copyright Morongwa Hope Moagi © 2017
All rights reserved.

Without limiting the rights under copyright, no part of this publication may be reproduced, stored in or introduced into a retrieval system, or transmitted, in any form, or by any means (electronic, mechanical, photocopying, recording, or otherwise) without the prior written permission of the copyright owner of this book.

Re ebook version: Thank you for respecting the author's work. An ebook is licensed for your personal use only whereas a paperback edition can be given away or re-sold. The ebook may not be re-sold or given away to other people. If you would like to share the ebook with another person, please download an additional copy for each person with whom you share it. If you are reading this as an ebook and did not purchase it, or it was not obtained for your use only, then you should obtain your own copy.

Teenage Thoughts of Hope

Biography

I am Morongwa Hope Moagi. I school at St George College which is located in Nkowankowa and I'm currently doing my grade ten. I was born on the 7th of April in 2002.
I live with both my parents and three siblings. I'm a fun-loving person and I believe I have a sweetheart nature. I'm not judgmental. I wish to become an optometrist or do something related to medicine.

My first poem was written in 2016 helped by Thabiso Rakgaole. My English teacher, Sir Ndou, led me to the road of literature and I've fallen in love with it and I've embraced it. Thanks Thabiso and you, my dear Sir.

Acknowledgements

Thanks to my parents for the support, my spiritual father, and most importantly my best friend Machukudu Maponya who always encouraged me to write and corrected some of my work.

Thanks to my publisher William Henry Jenkins for not giving up on me and this book, and thanks for the advice. I'm grateful.

Contents

Biography v
Acknowledgements vi
Betrayal 1
Love 3
Fake Friend 4
What is Perfection? 6
After I met you 8
Mother 10
I'm not perfect 12
Reaching for the skies 13
Yahweh is his name 15
Bitterness 17
Tiredness in a friendship 18
Be Careful 20
Failure 22
Love 24
Change is better when it's needed 25
Is succeeding the only thing in life? 26
Life 28
Kindness 29
Woman Supreme 31
The Pain of Loving Someone 33
Absent Father 34

Teenage Thoughts of Hope

Pain 36
Sister! 38
Editor 40

Betrayal

I didn't know what the word "betrayal" meant until a perfect gentleman decided to take me on a ride.

Well, I thank him for the experience and the lesson that he taught me.

I poured my heart out to him. I loved him, but I did not expect the worst betrayal from him. He made my life a living hell, yet I couldn't see it. I was blinded by love.

I never thought he would bring tears to my heart. He tore my heart into pieces. Remembering that they all warned me about him makes me feel bad. They said the exact things about who he really is. If I had listened to my friends and family, I would not have been the victim of his betrayal.

I trusted him; I loved him; I cared for him. His joy was my satisfaction, but he shattered me and broke me into pieces. He cut me deeper than a knife can. He made my world dark. He's just a great pretender.

Teenage Thoughts of Hope

Our life seemed to be more alive, but it was a big fat lie! He hated every moment he shared with me. He looked straight into my eyes and told me that he loved me.

Love? What is Love? Love is kind; love is patient; love does not boast; love is beautiful.

Well, I curse the day our eyes crossed each other's path.

I don't blame him. He's a coward.

I'm so glad to have seen his true colours before everything else happened. He left an unbearable pain and a wound nothing can heal.

Love

There I was thinking love was supposed to make me feel special and cared for. Well, it turns out I was wrong.

At first I thought I was lying to myself until I found love.

I loved you but what did you give me in return?

Pain, pain, oh unbearable pain.

I am a victim of a selfish kind of love.

There was a time when I knew my place in your heart, but now I don't know who you are. You made me want to attempt to do negative things, but my God was with me all the time.

Now I know why they say love them all, but trust no one. If only I had known with whom I was falling in love from the moment I set my eyes on you, I'd rewind time and wish I had never met you.

I'm hurt, but I will heal as times goes by.

Thanks for the lesson.

Fake Friend

Smile, kisses, you gave them to me.
We spent memorable days together.
I just never thought that you could turn out to be so heartless, cruel and so mean.

I shared my secrets with you, but you shared them with other people.

What kind of person are you?

You pretended to be my best friend and I believed you were, but all you ever wanted was information, all my secrets, even my weaknesses.

You told everyone everything I shared with you.

What a betrayal!

Everywhere I went people laughed at me, gave me weird looks and even called me all sorts of names.

The person they should be laughing at is you because you are bitter, a venomous snake and a fake.

But hey, it's all on me because I couldn't see the bitterness and fake in you.

I believed you were my shoulder to lean on.

I now see why they say "Love them all, but trust no one".

I'm a fool for trusting you.

From all this, I learned that there can never be anyone better than God.

A person like you can go extra miles and tell everyone my deepest weaknesses so as to be loved by the world, but Karma will be Karma and it has its own way of coming back to bite you.

What is Perfection?

What is perfection?

It is a state of being when becoming perfect.

It is the proficiency, skill or excellence as found in some forms of art.

What is perfection if there's nothing perfect?

The answer lies in the question itself. Since there's nothing perfect, this, in itself, is perfection.

Simply speaking, this world is imperfectly perfect.

I am not perfect; no one is perfect.
We are not perfect as human beings.
That is why we all need each other.

Every person has both weaknesses and strengths.

We need each other for the support on our weaknesses and for the compliments on our strengths.

I fear perfection, for once I tell myself I am

perfect, I can no longer have the enthusiasm to soldier on with what I am going to do.

I believe in the saying "There's always room for improvement".

Perfection implies Imperfection because once you tell yourself that everything you do and all you are is perfect, that is when that your perfectness becomes your imperfection. A perfect person does not know what improvement is.

In life, in order to learn, you have to fail. If you claim perfection, how then will you learn?

Perfect is a word used by those who feel they are better than others while actually, they are not.

Perfect is a word bandied around by people who think only about themselves, people who actually do not even know what perfection is.

Perfection is over-used in many cases.

Perfection puts limit on my personal safety. It is worthy of fear. I am not perfect and I fear perfection for it will isolate me from other people and from improvement.

After I met you

I always heard people saying that there are loyal friends out there, but I couldn't see them because I was in dreamland. I actually thought that being kind and sweet is all that people wanted to see in me. I always used to forgive each and every person even if they did wrong to me.

Love does blindfold people.

After I met you, I finally saw the world and all its people in a different perspective. I saw the cruelty of the people of this planet. I guess that's called being in the real world.

In you I saw that it's not compulsory for me to have many more friends than enemies because then I wouldn't have more blessings that I have. You taught me that "one man for himself and God to us all" simply means that I shouldn't rely on other people because doing that can isolate me from happiness.

In you I learned that loyalty is key. I learned that no matter how much people neglect you, you do not have to lose your faith. It's the only thing that's going to keep you up.

Teenage Thoughts of Hope

In you I also learned that I should not misinterpret or think people's smiles actually mean they love me because not everybody is a saint.

In you I also learned the courage to be hated and laughed at because not everyone will love me.

Mother

It is said that a mother is one of the most important sources of happiness and, believe me, my happiness lies in her smile.

You are a beauty with a sweetheart nature. You are so fit and flexible. You decided to carry me for nine full months and you did not complain about losing your figure. You went through labour pains and too much craving of food and yet you never complained.

You are worthy of everything because not only are you my mother but also you are my best friend. In you I find my resting place and my place of comfort. We may have arguments now and then, but never do you cross my mind and heart because you are the woman that no other woman can be.

You were there when I took my first baby step and when I actually got to say my first word which was "Mommy". I now see why that was my first word. You are a unique woman in all ways. You always picked me up and comforted me every time I fell. I gave you sleepless nights and yet you never complained, but gave me pure love.

Teenage Thoughts of Hope

I can never thank you enough.

I'm not perfect and yet you choose to love me.

I'm so blessed to have you in my life. To the world, you may be nothing special, but to me you are My World. I love you; you and only you.

Your name is special in every way. You are a true beauty with a beauty that never fades. You are my everything. I know you'll always remain a great Mom and my best friend ever.

Ain't no momma that's gonna take your place!

I'm not perfect

As for me, I'm not perfect, but you'll never find anyone else like me.

I'm not perfect, but I assure you, you will never find another loving, caring and a sweet-hearted nature like mine. I may have my flaws, but I'm unique.

I may not have it all, but a soul which is as pure as mine, is one you will search for everywhere, but never find.

I may do things that are unpopular and may be rude sometimes, but, believe me, I'm one of a kind, one of God's precious gifts.

I may have friends that pair with me in everything, but you won't find me in them because I'm me and I will always remain me for as long as I live.

I may be disliked by many people and I may be spoken badly about by other people, but, believe me, peoples' opinions don't matter to me.

I am not perfect, but you will never find someone else like me.

Reaching for the skies

I've always lived under the words "Will I ever reach them?" I always thought that one day I would reach the skies because I didn't believe that the sky is the limit.

My world was a place of doubt because I didn't think I could see things in a different perspective.

I've always lived under peoples' shoulders because I was afraid of seeing the people of this world. It made my life a cartoon network.

I always would "lay low" because I was afraid of what I would experience in this world, but one thing I forgot was that I should reach for the skies for there lies my comfort zone.

People have always put me down, but still I rose.

I may have been to the most dangerous place where I was told I would never make it back alive.

I may have been defeated, but I am still reaching for the skies.

I may lack love and money and all the beautiful

things of this cruel world, but one thing I know is that I am never going to stop rising. My goal to reach the skies won't let me stop. Instead, it will make me rise for I'm a riser and a defeat defeater.

Yahweh is his name

He is a faithful God and he is the God who never sleeps.

He is worthy of all the praises because he is the pillar of every person's life.

It is said that he is that God who answers every person's prayer.

Truly, his name is Yahweh for he is bigger than everything in the world, for he is Jehovah jairah, for he is Jehovah nisi, for he is Jehovah Adonai, the master of everything.

Nnete ke kgosi ya di kgosi (Truly he is the king of kings), ke morena wa marena (he is the Lord of Lord's).

In him we find our homes, comfort zones, a world full of butterflies and peace, for he is the Lord of miracles.

As Lebo Sekgobela says "ndaka chiangetedzwa" (in him we are safe).

In him we find a mother, father and a king whose name is Yahweh.

He is the maker of heaven and earth. If it were not for his love and affection, his caring for us, we wouldn't be glowing as we are today.

He is the Lord that forgives and forgets; the Lord that never hates, but loves.

It is written that he is a jealous God. He reminds me of MTN because he is everywhere we go and he is always here for us.

He reigns forever; he is the lion of Judah.

As Charles Jenkins says "My God is awesome. He can move mountains. He keeps me in the valley and hides me from the rain. My God is awesome. He heals where I've been broken, strengthens where I've been weakened. Forever he'll reign."

Yes, he is right because God is greater than any deity that's ever existed.

Nnete o dutse setulong sa bokgosi. (He is seated on the chair of his royal highness, Yahweh.)

I love Sipho Ngwenya because he says "Jesus came in the morning when the people thought they were done with you at night; he came in the morning to give new power".

Bitterness

I have been to the worst, far from the better and I've struggled to accept my broken heart.

I cursed the day I met you. You seemed to be a decent person, one who could never harm even a fly, but how was I to know the bitterness within you.

I curse the day you brought shame and hatred upon my heart. I don't know how to love anymore and it's all because of your stupid, inconsiderate actions. I gave myself to you, but what I got in return was not what I had expected. As they say "great expectations often lead to great disappointments". You brought more meaning to that.

I cried and cried, but it seemed that my cry was not loud enough for you to come and comfort me. Why do you do bad things? You know that I'm human and I've got feelings too. Why is it that your heart contains more evil than good?

Truly speaking, I shouldn't have judged you before getting to know you better, but how was I to know you would shatter me into pieces. Sepedi se re "go se tsebe ke kotse". (Sometimes not knowing something is a crime.)

Tiredness in a friendship

It's as if I'm locked away from the only thing that belongs to me, my life. I feel as if I'm not in control of my own life.

I'm not free at all because I'm afraid my master will think I've changed on him.

I always have to seek permission whenever I decide to do something because I'm afraid I'll later be left alone.

Mary says "nobody told me the road would be easy", but believe me, I'm seeing sorrows which can never fade in my heart and mind.

I had a perfect, free life until I could no longer control it.

I've always given away my loved ones just to plead for a risky friendship, but now it's over. It's time I controlled what I've been putting on hold for a person not worthy of being a part of my life.

I can now stand tall in front of my so-called friend and tell her what's on my nerves because now I have the courage to do so.

Teenage Thoughts of Hope

I was trapped in the "amazing world of gumball", but I think it's time I slipped out of the world of no peace, the world of no understanding, the world not fit for kind people, the world full of sharks, and go to a world full of possibilities.

A message to all kind people, innocent people: do not let people rule the only life that you can control; do not be kind to those who do not even deserve your kindness; always open your eyes.

The world is full of sharks who want to swallow you.

Be Careful

Be careful of the person sitting next you.

Be careful of the thoughts that are sitting in your head.

Be careful of the words your friend is telling you.

Be careful because this life we live has no beginning and no end.

Be careful is a word that should never cross your mind while doing things because we people tend to forget that the devil was once an angel before he wronged God, so what can a human being be?

Remember that not all that glitters is gold. This simply means that not everyone is going to want to see you happy. Only a few will. One thing I'm certain about is that some people are definitely going to wear smiles on their faces, but deep down in their hearts they are waiting for your downfall so that they can celebrate. Those people are hypocrites.

Teenage Thoughts of Hope

If you don't like a person, it is better to show it to their face than it is to pretend that you like them.

Be careful for you don't know what a person is planning against you.

Wake up and face reality because we are in a world where everyone is being kind to be cruel, where a person has to make more enemies than friends.

Be careful for the world is a cruel place. The world is one bad place because everyone seems to do things to fit in with the world's edition, but, believe me, they end up becoming the edition so soon that they lose their value very fast. My dear, be careful of that.

Be careful not to be fooled by the word "love" because it is wrong coming from a person who doesn't even know the value of love.

Keep your eyes open at all times and always stay awake.

Be careful for we are in a world full of sharks, so be careful not to be swallowed.

Failure

Failure to me is a motivation because if you don't fail in life, you don't know life.

People might define failure in many ways, but I define it as a building block to something great, success in many other things.

In life, we go through different situations and meet obstacles, but I call those tests which actually make us strong.

Failure makes you realize what you've done wrong and then encourages you to be above it because you are aware of and want to avoid having the same problem again.

A failure, to me, is not different from a mistake because if I make a mistake, I am going to actually learn from it. This works with failure, too.

I am not afraid of failure because it's proof that I was not working hard enough on the main point, and I should work harder next time.

Failure is a building block to something great.

Teenage Thoughts of Hope

Never be afraid of failure for it gives you a second chance to be above it.

Love

Love is a wonderful thing. It's something so special that comes only at a certain time.

Love coming from someone who does not know love can kill you.

Never hope high in terms of a love relationship because it is said that great expectations often lead to disappointments that make you feel rejected and that is the most painful thing ever.

Love, but do not love too deeply; hope, but do not set your hopes too high.

People often say "to love is to be and to be is to love", but loving a person may kill you in a way that hurts the most. Do not love too deeply, because if you do and your trust gets betrayed, your heart breaks.

Always remember that true love is rare.

Change is better when it's needed

Realize how easy it is to change from how much you used to love someone to hating or despising that person.

My point is that no matter how much your relationship with a person is worth to you, it's always an easy thing to change. It's not right trying to change a person who wants the best for you, but who shows it in another way, maybe in a way that you don't like. Still, don't try to change the person or question their actions.

People may go all out to make you feel happy, but eventually you find out that was not really what they wanted to do. They made you happy only to please you. When that love is questioned, trust fades slowly.

Change is an easy thing to do.

You don't have to change something you think is not right when you know it is right. Always take your feelings seriously because they can tell you whether or not something is right.

Change is better only when it's needed.

Is succeeding the only thing in life?

Succeeding is the very best thing in life, right? But is succeeding the only good thing in life?

I find it hard to believe that without success you are like a paper unwritten because I know and believe that all that you need in life is God. So how are you unwritten whilst there is a God?

The Bible says seek first the Kingdom of God and then the rest shall fall in place.

Your success is a very great thing, but not compared to what you can do and be. God is a multi-tasker. He knew the plans he had for you before you were even begotten and He also knew that you were going to succeed, but how is it that when you do not have success you are nothing?

It makes no sense because God is above everything in this entire world and therefore that makes him the most powerful and greatest person on earth and in heaven.

They say that "education is the most powerful weapon to success", but God shows up and it turns out that God is the most powerful person behind every success. You can be successful, but, without God, you become a full book with unwritten pages.

Seek first the Kingdom of God and the rest shall fall in place.

Bear in mind that success is not success without God.

Life

What is life? Life is a journey of tests and it's indeed a journey with no destination.

People often say that life is hard, but to face reality, life becomes hard when you have nothing to live for and you live according to other people's expectations.

Life is full of tests which are often failed by people who try to be who they are not and not who they are.

In order for life to be meaningful, you have to experience every tragedy life gives you; then you'll be so very strong that nothing can ever bring you down.

The tests in life actually make you stronger despite the fact that they might be tests which weigh you down, but at the end of the day you'll have to pull yourself together because you know that the tests you face are not permanent.

Friends are going to come and go, but all there's to do is always to beware of the extent to which friends can go to actually betray you.

Life is the greatest gift of all. Take care of it.

Kindness

Giving back to a community is not an easy thing to do because it takes courage. Giving and caring for people is an extraordinary thing to do. It becomes more special when it comes from within because there's no greater gift than the one that comes from within.

There's a sepedi proverb which says "letsogo le lengwe le hlatswa le lengwe". This simply means that one hand helps the other and together, as human beings, we have to help one another.

There are many ways of helping people. Help can be in the form of advising a certain person or giving the needy something they lack.

I often used to say that not all people deserve your kindness; only the ones who are actually your friends deserve it. Then, one day a small kid actually showed me the importance of being kind.

Your kindness can make a very huge impact on another person's life. It may not mean much to you, but it could mean the world to other people. Having a chat with a kid about kindness changed a part of me and I came to know that advice can make you see a certain issue in a better way. It can change a person's thinking completely.

Help other people and you will be offered the same help, perhaps in a different way.

Your love and care can change a person completely.

Kindness is a gift and it should be used for betterment.

Woman Supreme

She is a woman so strong that she's become unshakeable, so wise that no one competes with her. She just wants to be a woman who is destined for greater things. She wants to be a woman who will not let her past be the determiner of her great and bright future.

She was born in a dusty village and even today she has never stopped walking on the red sand. She never complains about the dust because deep within the midst of the dust lies a great woman who was able to put everything aside and focus on the one thing that gave her life, God.

She is a woman full of talents, but she never brags about how good she is. She encourages people to live a life which they know is theirs, rather than live a life which others choose for them.

Through it all, she was able to put her happiness first instead of having to plead with others who meant nothing to her.

Women are obsessed with changing the color of their skin and some wear the world's latest fashions, but a woman with dignity wears something that's more proper or that goes with her morals. She does not need makeup to be who she is.

Alexia Cara says "there's no a better you than the you that you are". By this she means that you don't have to change yourself for anyone; you should be yourself.

Through it all, remember that women who have morals and good values are worth a thousand of those who do not.

Be you, do you, for you.

Be your own woman supreme.

The Pain of Loving Someone

It pains me to know you're a coward.
You never show me your love,
Yet you want us to go forward.
Is it because you are scared to love?

Actions speak louder than words,
Believe me yours are quite clear.
You have taught me that you can be loved,
But few get your love returned here.

Do I shame you? Am I not enough?
Are you happy to see me in tears?
If I cannot meet your high standards?
I won't be changed in the years.

It pains me to think you were better,
Than all of the rest of the men.
It pains me to know you are dismal.
By chance can I change you again?

I love you, however it's paining,
I'm starting to love you some more.
It pains me that we are not meant to be,
But dammit I loved you before.

Absent Father

I've always wondered how much a father could do in one's life, but the answer to my question is not here, because I don't happen to have a caring dad. I am just an ordinary girl with a mother, but no one to call "Daddy".

I had always wished for my dad to be there every time I fell down, to comfort me and to tell that everything will be alright. I wished to have experienced the daddy and daughter moments. I had never imagined that lacking a father would make me feel unwanted and I'd never had the chance to think about it until now because suddenly I'm all grown up and now need the guidance of a father. I need a father to look me in the eyes and tell me that there's never going to be a man who will love me as he does.

I would love to know who you were, what you liked, what you did for a living, what you loved and what you didn't love. Why can't I feel your love as a daughter? I might not be the only child, but I'm definitely the one child who needs a father's love and someone to call daddy.

I used to ask mother where you were, but I've come to realize that asking her that was actually tearing her apart by reminding her of you. I know that life is unpredictable and it tears me down to know my dad died before knowing me.

I know you look out for me from where ever you are. I've come to learn that God is the father to the fatherless.

My dear absent Father, I love you!

Pain

What is pain?

Pain is an unpleasant feeling caused by injury or illness. Pain can be caused in many ways. It can be caused by discomfort and therefore can cause suffering or distress to a person.

Pain is not only a physical thing, but it can also be in the form of emotional issues leading to distress and many other things. Distress is caused by worry or exhaustion.

You know you are in pain only when you've lost something valuable. It becomes a problem when you cannot move on without that valuable thing.

People come and go in our lives, but you have to be grateful for the ones that stay.

People are there either to build you or to destroy you.

Pain is in knowing that although there's something missing in your life, the odds aren't in your favor that you can do anything about it.

Pain reminds you that you shouldn't trust too much for paining someone takes only a few minutes, perhaps seconds.

Pain leaves a scar in one's life. Once that scar is left, it's hard to move on.

Pain is greatly felt in the heart for the heart is the most sensitive part of the human body.

Sister!

We argue; we laugh; we get jealous with each other; we get angry about the most trivial things; we pretend to be cool around parents, but when left alone we shout at each other.

Okay!

However, we are sisters united by love and there's nothing that can break a sister's bond.

Through it all, the toughest situations, the most weird pains, you were there and are still here to support me. Through thick and thin you showed me that no matter how many times we fight, it doesn't matter because where love is concerned all things fall into place.

In my sad days you always manage to put a smile on my face and in my happiest days you always manage to make sure you spoil my mood, but I've become used to the way we sisters act towards each other.

The most important thing that you taught me was to appreciate the little that God gave me. You taught me that it's God first and the rest shall fall into place. You also taught me the importance of prayer. If there's something I'm grateful for, it has to be helping me find God. I'm forever grateful. Indeed, a sister you are!

A goddess you are, a young lady full of laughter. I call you my sister. No matter how many times you fight with someone, remember when love exists, problems and differences don't matter.

Editor

Mr. William Jenkins was born in Ottawa, Canada in 1932. He became a computer programmer and worked in that field for 45 years. Subsequently, he sold residential real estate and then wrote and published a few mystery stories for middle-school children.

After finding publishing using Createspace particularly easy, he began publishing books for others as a free service. There is no charge for the publishing and editing service. See his website

http://williamjenkins.ca.

He is especially interested in publishing stories and poems from students. A few students from South Africa have submitted their writing.

If you are a teacher or student, submit your writing to **williamhenryjenkins@gmail.com**.

www.ingramcontent.com/pod-product-compliance
Lightning Source LLC
Chambersburg PA
CBHW060936050426
42453CB00009B/1034